ROXANNE LOWIT

PHOTOGRAPHS

YVES SAINT LAURENT

FOREWORD BY PIERRE BERGÉ

JERRY HALL
VALERIE STEELE
PAT CLEVELAND
GRACE JONES
BETTY CATROUX
PALOMA PICASSO
CATHERINE DENEUVE
LUCIE DE LA FALAISE

SHARE YSL MOMENTS

Foreword by Pierre Bergé: Following Yves Saint Laurent's considerably successful exhibition at New York's Metropolitan Museum of Art, and just as he was about to board the Concorde to return to Paris, Roxanne Lowit appeared out of nowhere, placed a big cardboard model of the Empire State Building into his arms, and took the picture that was to become so well-known. After having shown some of his work in New York, Yves was immortalized kissing one of the most famous symbols of the city. I tell this story to show that Roxanne is always there, even when she is not expected. Her sharp eye has been able to capture the most secret situations, the most hidden of mysteries. This book shows that nothing is less objective than a lens. Roxanne chooses her subjects, scrutinizes them, lays them bare, and allows each one of us to reach a moment of truth.

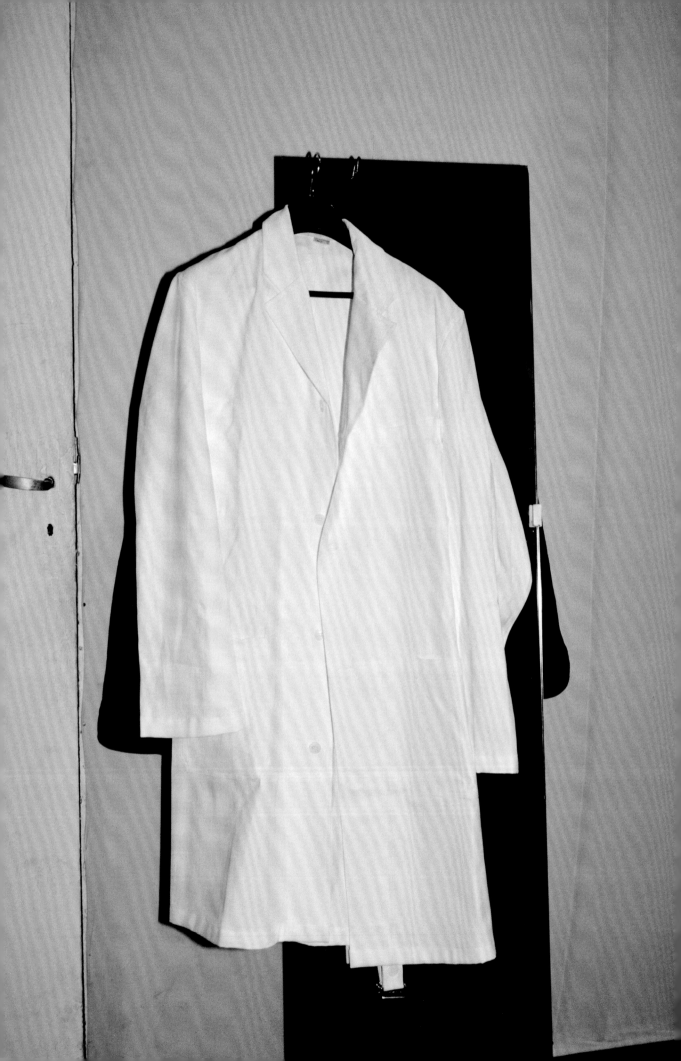

Roxanne Lowit: I love *Yves Saint Laurent.* His name is synonymous with style, elegance and high fashion. I love that I met him on top of the **Eiffel Tower**. I love that I always felt welcomed backstage. I loved that he had such a passion for his work. I loved his vision. I loved how detail-oriented and hands-on he was, making sure every girl was **perfect**, standing there in his white lab coat inspecting them as they exited onto the runway. It was a privilege to watch his creative process. I love how his designs **empowered women**, focusing on their strengths. I love his tuxedo; it transformed women's evening wear. I love that I was his photographer for the Metropolitan Museum of Art's "Yves Saint Laurent, 25 Years of Design" exhibit. I love that I called him "Yves" even though everyone else called him "Monsieur Saint Laurent." I loved his aura: strong yet vulnerable. I loved how passionate he was about his work. He was *brilliant.* I loved how his models reflected beauty across the spectrum. I loved that from the beginning he put the "**Heart**," a piece of jewelry based on an early drawing of his, on his favorite ensemble show after show, year after year. I loved that the "Heart" was always delivered by his driver *in a shoebox.* I loved that though he was extremely shy, backstage he was in his element, joyful and confident. I love that he had a silly side. I loved that he was relaxed and comfortable around me. I loved that he trusted me, and my camera. I love that he *inspired* me to find my calling. I love that whether surrounded by a bevy of beauties or peeking out to see the models on the catwalk, every moment was a joyous photo op for me. I love sharing these **magical** moments with the world so they may see *Yves Saint Laurent* **through my eyes**

*From Texas to Couture by Jerry Hall: I had barely left Texas when I found myself modeling Haute Couture for Yves Saint Laurent. It was the beginning of a great relationship. I count my lucky stars that I was able to work with him for so many years. I might have been too exotic for Texas, but not **too exotic** to be the Opium girl for eight years, starting when YSL first launched the perfume in 1977. During that time I got to travel the world with him promoting the perfume. It was, of course, **très chic** and a total hoot! I got to see so many wonderful places and things. One of the most memorable was watching Rudolf Nureyev dancing the Faun. Yves was a **darling**, **gentle** man, who always wanted everyone around him to be **happy**. He was very generous, often giving us models the clothes we wore in the shows. I still have most of the clothes he gave me, except for a few that I donated to a benefit. Yves was a **perfectionist**, with an incredible eye for detail. He was very **hands-on**: he would fix my hair and tie on bows or belts. There was nothing too big or too small for him to do himself. I am so grateful that I was fortunate enough to have spent so much time with this sweet, kind and **wonderfully** talented man.*

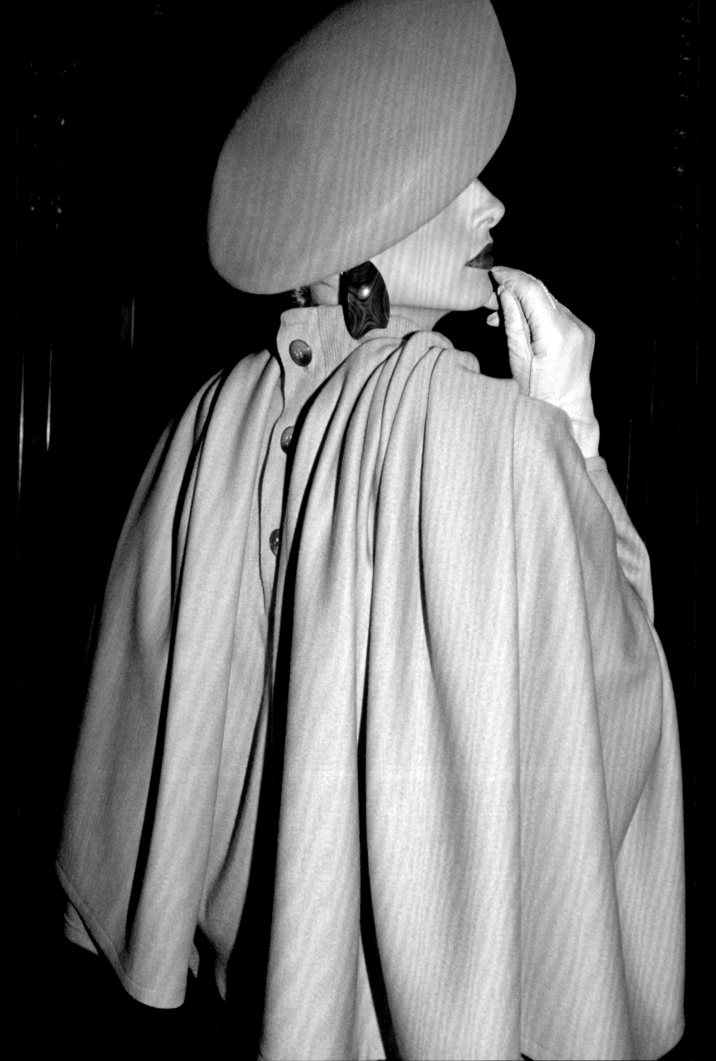

Valerie Steele: Roxanne Lowit has photographed thousands of fashion shows, parties, and celebrities. Yet her work on Yves Saint Laurent stands out for its visual splendor and historic importance. One of the most influential designers of the twentieth century, Yves Saint Laurent was a veritable Picasso of the fashion world, whose deep font of creativity made him the most influential designer of his era. However, it is not only his brilliance as an artist which inspired Roxanne. She also felt a deep affinity for him as a human being. Roxanne likes to recall how she first met Saint Laurent (together with Andy Warhol) on top of the Eiffel Tower. Not only was this meeting extremely exciting and glamorous for Roxanne, it also confirmed for the neophyte photographer that she was on the right path for her career. Later, when Saint Laurent came to New York City for his exhibition at the Metropolitan Museum of Art, Roxanne became his official photographer, documenting his triumphal visit. In Roxanne's new book, we see Saint Laurent, smiling as he listens to the grande dame of fashion, Diana Vreeland, at the opening of his exhibition. We see him, smiling again, surrounded by his proud and delighted models, and we see him, looking impossibly young and handsome, at a gala dinner with his friend Paloma Picasso. We see fashion models like Jerry Hall, striding along the runway, and, again, fooling around backstage, torso naked between a ruffled bra top and a ruffled skirt. Many pictures, of course, remind us that it was Roxanne who pioneered the now-ubiquitous genre of backstage fashion photography, which gives us all an insider's view of fashion. And if everyone looks their most beautiful, that is a tribute to the warm regard with which Roxanne is held by all the subjects of her camera. There will never be another Yves Saint Laurent, but long may Roxanne Lowit keep photographing the world of fashion!

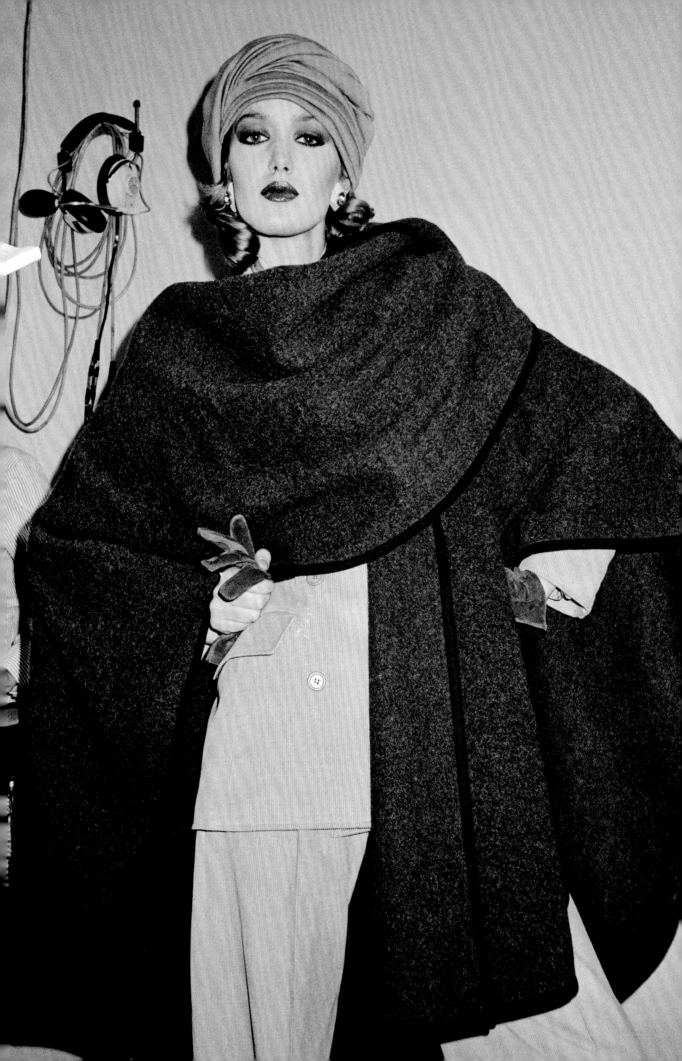

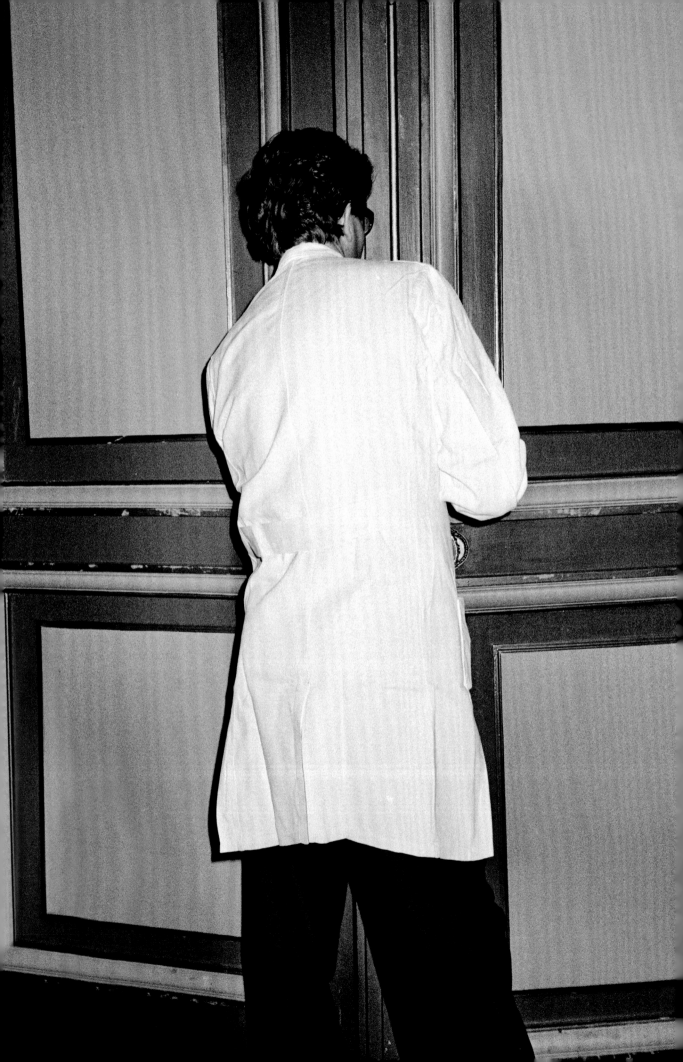

Pat Cleveland: *I came in contact with Yves Saint Laurent's creations when I was fifteen. At that time I was modeling for the Ebony Fashion Fair; there was a show every night for three months in which I modeled Yves Saint Laurent clothes. I loved this one dress which had a nude appliqué of a woman's body on it. When I appeared on the stage, people would think that I was nude, until I turned around so they could see that it was in fact a dress. The dress always got applause. It would be years before I would meet Yves personally. In 1970 I went to Paris to join up with Antonio Lopez, the illustrator. The first time I ever set eyes on Yves Saint Laurent was in the summer of 1971, when Antonio was invited to Yves's défilé. Of course, Antonio had to take his gang along, which included Juan Ramos, Donna Jordan, Corey Tippin and me. We were so excited and dressed to be seen at the show. That's what one did. On the way to the show I was crossing the street with the gang when this*

Volkswagen Beetle came speeding by, then it came to a screeching halt just in front of the building where *the show* would be. Out of the car stepped this tall, thin, refined-looking young man. He wore a dark, well-fitted suit and oversize black square-rimmed glasses. It was Yves. I was **starstruck** seeing him for the first time, and in a **flash** he had hurried off to his own show. That same summer the gang and I decided to have our hair dry brushed in this special secret salon. And there was Yves, just like us getting powdered and dry brushed. It was funny to watch all of us sitting there peeking at each other in the mirrors with clouds of white powder whiffing through the air— we all had lots of hair in those days. In the same period I was doing a lot of editorial work traveling. In between jobs I would go out thinking I was incognito wearing a poncho and jeans. One day I was walking down a small street by boulevard Saint-Germain when I heard a voice call my name from a balcony.

above. "Pat! Pat! Come up!" It was Fernando Sanchez, a designer friend from New York, and next to him stood Yves . . . Well, I went up, and over cucumber sandwiches and champagne mimosas, I got to know Yves . . . It was pure joy, with the storytelling about their adventures in Morocco. It was Yves who convinced me on that day that I should stay in the "World of Fashion" and not run off and get lost somewhere. Yves said in his quiet way, "We need you to show our clothes." Well, I took his word for it and stayed on track . . . In that winter of 1971, I was called personally by Yves to fit for his défilé. The great thing was to be greeted at Yves's salon. It was like magic when you were allowed to go through the large doors, up the marble stairs into the showroom, which looked as if it could be the lobby of a Grand Hotel with its plush carpets and tufted round sofa chairs covered in a deep red velvet; there were golden-rimmed pillars and great rainbow-catching chandeliers. Finally, where I had to go was through these black lacquered doors to a small passage which led to the cabine, where the world would disappear and the competition would start. Most of Yves's models were very serious—their lives depended on this job, and so did mine in a way. There were few words spoken and lots of preening in front of the makeup mirrors. In the cabine one felt like a doll in the box waiting to be unwrapped. The cabine was like a tall, narrow dressing closet with built-in hanging areas up to the ceiling along the right side. On the left side were the vanity mirrors surrounded by hundreds of lightbulbs. Everyone in the dressing room would wait in silence for Yves to arrive, then there would be a rush of excitement. "Monsieur Yves has arrived!" Suddenly everyone came to life, the dressers started to rush me, practically tearing off my clothes, shouting "Vite! Vite!" They would pull off my stockings, put on my stockings, fix the seams in my stockings, while someone would be pulling something over my head, as I would be stuck in a turtleneck collar, holding my breath under the tissue paper which they have put over my head so as not to dirty the clothes with makeup—the paper would melt between my *lips*—all of this action in a brief *eternal moment*, then I'd be freed and dressed and quickly pushed out of the door of the cabine into the grand room of the master designer. I stood there in stocking feet on the plush silk carpet. There were tables laid out with trays of sparkling *jewels* which bedazzled my senses. I was then guided towards a row of beautiful high-heeled platform shoes, an assistant put a pair on me—which elevated me to nine inches taller—then I was led like a stallion to just under the giant chandelier in the center of the room, where I was to be accessorized. Finally I was standing still, where I could see a wall of two-story-high French windows with their heavy silk drapes fringed and tasseled with tiebacks, and there, sitting quietly, almost invisible, in the front row of these tiny golden chairs was Yves, wearing a white worker's jacket, one hand in his pocket and the other holding a cigarette. He gave a quiet, knowing smile as his eyes started to twinkle through his heavy-framed glasses, as though inspiration had come to him; he took one last long puff of his cigarette, as though he were lingering in some sort of dream world, then he jumped up with a burst of energy. Looking at the garment, he walked all the way around me. "How are you?" he says, in English with a French accent, in a quiet, humble voice. I wanted to say "I feel I'm in heaven just being near you," but I said very quietly, "Happy." Slowly a smile rises in him as it does in me from the depths of my soul, and in his quiet way he starts to bejewel me slowly, carefully, knowingly, starting at the neck, then the wrists, till every possible place left on me is covered in jewels . . . And from that time onward, I became one of Yves's mannequins. What a blessing

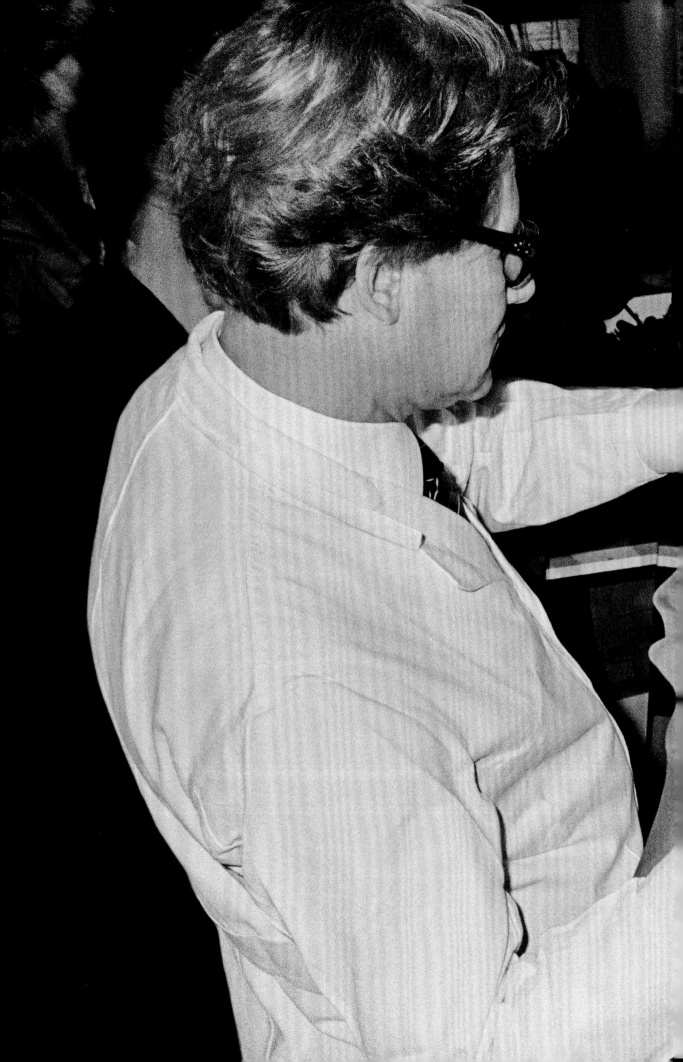

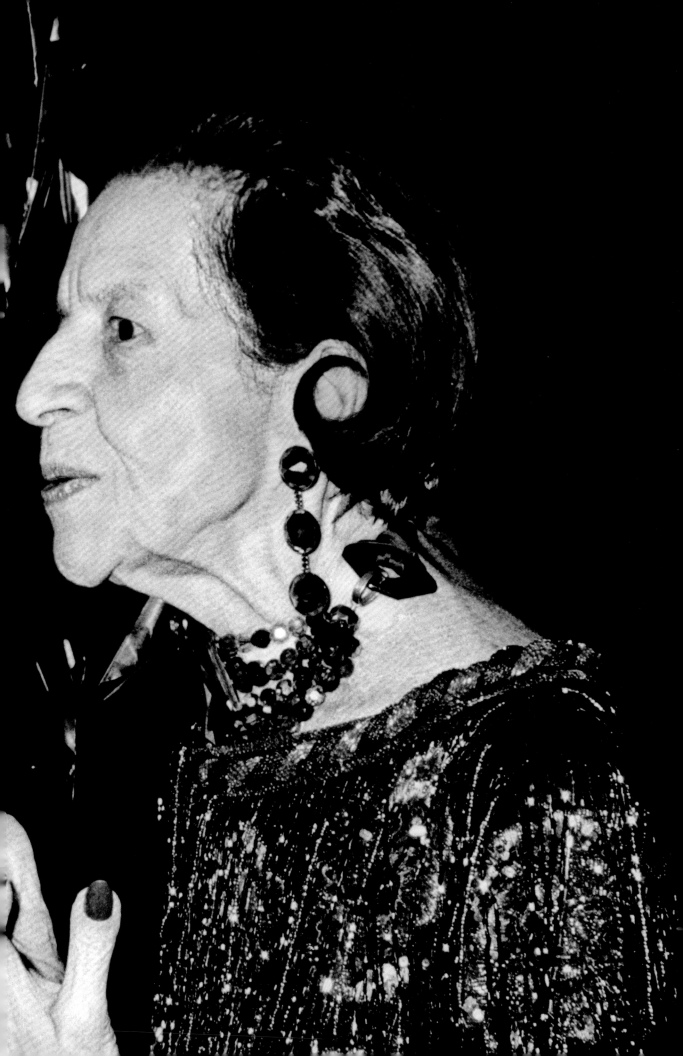

Grace Jones: I remember when the Palace opened, walking from the stage thinking I could get to the balcony and sing from there. By the time I got there all my clothes were torn off by fans. The lights were turned down and I still had to sing "la Vie en Rose," which they were all waiting for. Luckily for me, Saint Laurent and Loulou were watching from the wings. He said, "You cannot go on naked," so he took off his tuxedo cummerbund, put it around my breasts, and draped Loulou's scarf on my hips like an Egyptian belly dancer. I was lifted back onto the stage on the shoulders of my dancer. The rest is history.

Betty Catroux: Yves picked me up in a nightclub and we never left each other and spent a fairy-tale life together, full of fun and beauty. He gave me everything in every sense. It was magic and it still is . . .

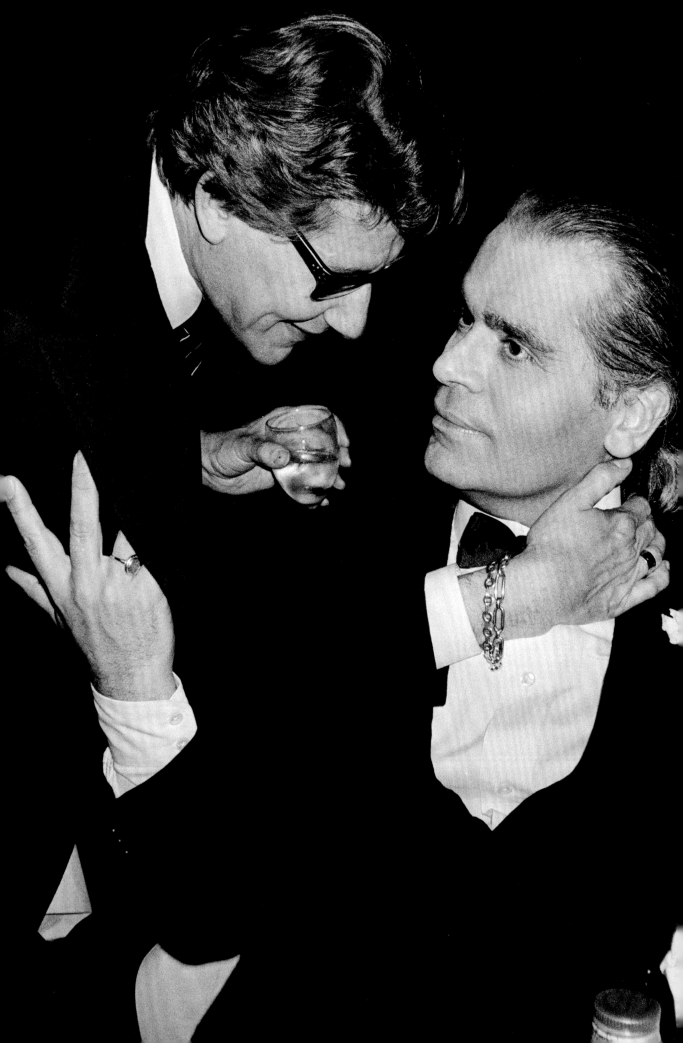

Paloma Picasso: When I met Yves, fashion wasn't yet the fashionable event and business it is today. Of course, there was a sense of *anticipation* and *excitement*, you might have had Catherine Deneuve, Hélène Rochas and Lauren Bacall sitting on the first row, but basically things were very tame at the Couture House, rue Spontini. It was just about the clients and a few professionals, all very **chic** and composed. Yves was very influential in **changing** the world of fashion by creating the Rive Gauche collections and boutiques, making creative designs accessible to a wider and younger audience. I can remember my own fascination at discovering the safari jacket and the tuxedo on Betty Catroux in the pages of Vogue: **sexy** in a totally new way, totally modern without being modernistic. Young people like me could relate to Couture thanks to him. We met in Paris. I was hiding all evening under a large fedora, both being shy we exchanged only a few words. From then on, I managed to be invited to see his collections, which was such a privilege. Returning from London with what I thought was the find of the century—a 1940s Gloria Swanson kind of a dress from the Portobello Market—I dressed up one evening in this and a pink turban with feathers that I had convinced a friend of my mother to give me and ran into Yves at dinner. It sparked his imagination in a special way, bringing back memories of his elegant mother's outfits in Oran during the war years. The next day, he started designing the glamorous broad-shouldered suggestive dresses and fur coats that created an *uproar* during the press previews. It was turning into a *scandal*. Pierre [Bergé] asked me and Loulou de La Falaise to come to the show to sound out the reaction of the public. I was wearing my dress in a less flamboyant styling—after all it was only 10 a.m.! *Ultimately*, it took fashion out into the broadsheets, creating an unheard-of and unbelievable international *buzz*. Yves once surprised me with a **Picasso** collection. I went on to pose in some of those dresses, which were truly *fabulous*. My father had dedicated himself to reworking Old Master paintings, in particular Velázquez's "Las Meninas." In these paintings, as in others, he included details of garments as significant messages, so he would have enjoyed this turn of events! The blossoming of ready-to-wear was even more stunning, as it went from showings in front of buyers at the "no glamour" Mendes headquarters, rue d'Aboukir, to the huge flower-filled tents of the Jardins du Palais-Royal, which accommodated glitterati of all kinds and ever-growing crowds fighting to attend. One tended to go to the Couture shows with more expectation than the **RTW**, on the presupposition that Yves had more freedom, less pressure. One that was particularly impressive was the Carmen collection; it must have been 1976, at the same time as the **Ballets Russes** and **Opera** collections. To the music of Carmen by Bizet, Yves presented a fantastic and inventive play on a theatrical gypsy look, high-lighted by a flower behind the ear. I felt this was the perfect collection for me! I was enthralled—the mix of Spanish references, bright red, white and black, laced-up corsets, bouffant skirts, operatic exuberance marked by the recurring apparition of an Escamillo played by a male model dressed as a toreador. The show went on and on, more outfits kept pouring onto the **catwalk** just when you thought you were reaching the grand finale, the toreador would appear again and it would start over with more models dazzling us. The climax of any collection is always the presentation of the bride, and the one that still outshines all the others for me was the regal widow bride, with her two ladies-in-waiting also dressed in black, as were the pages. It was **absolutely breathtaking!** Yves was forever creating magic on the runway, building to a crescendo of emotions that somehow overwhelmed us and brought tears to our eyes. Yet his eye for beauty and style extended far beyond the catwalk. I remember going to Château Gabriel in Normandy and finding my magazines disappearing from my room as Yves regarded them as disrupting the perfection of the décor! Anybody who met Yves fell **under his spell.** He seemed like an angel and yet he was maybe more like a mischievous child testing the limits—an incredibly gifted child with an artistic mind. He had a **special aura** that made all who approached him want to be his favorite, but **beauty** was his only master and it was sacred to him.

Catherine Deneuve: I met Yves Saint Laurent through work. I had a lot of fittings with him because he dressed me for so many different films. Because of this I had the chance to get close to him. I suppose I am not the first to say he was very shy. Sometimes his shyness was a bit innocent, like a child, and like a child he liked to have fun. It was such a big deal, what he was doing; he was under a lot of pressure and there were a lot of expectations of him. So he would kid around, you know—something light and very silly. He had a great sense of humor. He designed many clothes for me, at first mostly for my films, but he also did clothes for me when I had events to attend like the Cannes Film Festival. It was really special. When he designed something specifically for me, they were always elegant and sophisticated clothes. Very feminine. I was doing films and I was going out, being seen. There was a period where you would dress in Couture even during the day. Things have changed since then. He is not here anymore, so things have changed. Though the basis of our relationship was professional, there was an amitié as well. Some-times I would go with him to these big events at the Opéra or wherever. Just the fact that I was there with him, near him, he would be more comfortable. When I went to his last show, I sang for him at the end of the show. I was very nervous but I did it. For him,

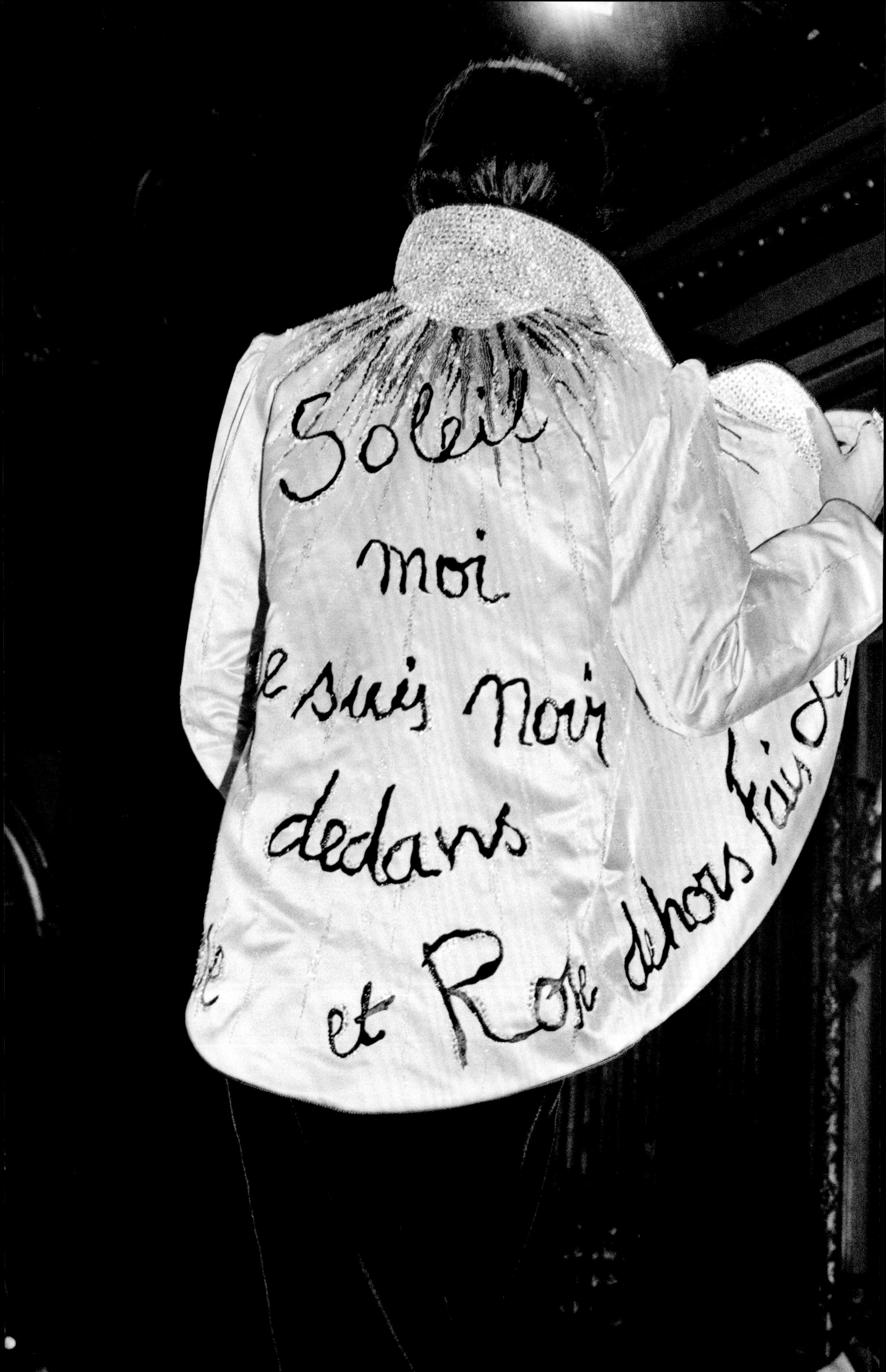
Soleil
moi
suis Noir
dedans
et Rose dehors

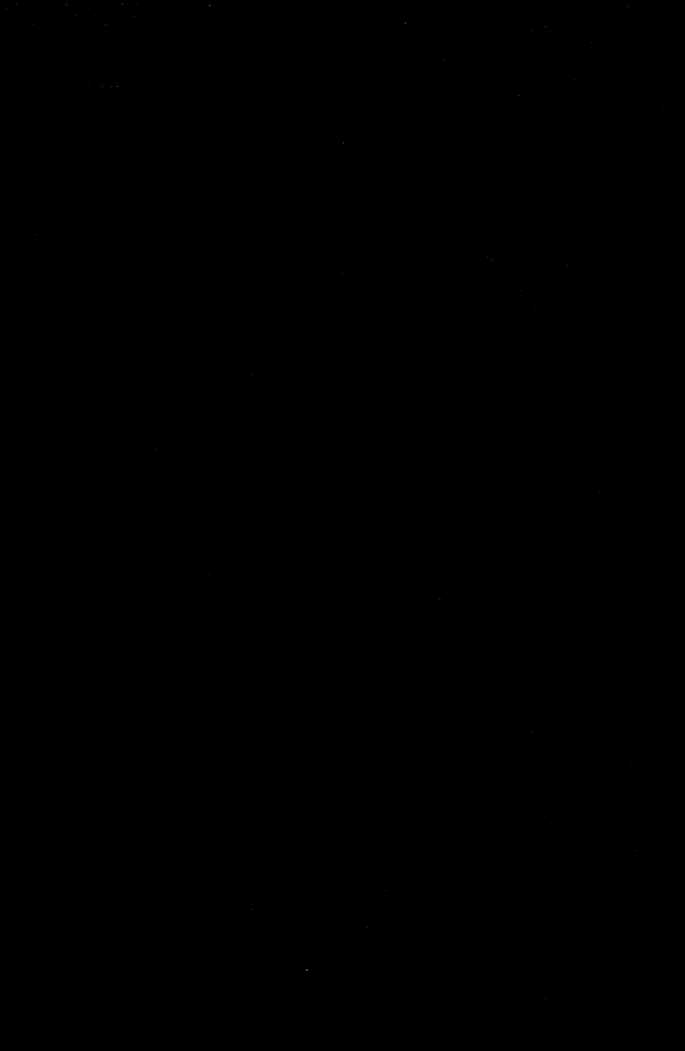

Yves and Loulou by Lucie de La Falaise:
My first memory of Yves is when I was four years old in 1977. I had been invited by Loulou to join Yves at the avenue Marceau design studio. Yves kindly asked me if I would like him to make me a fairy dress, so of course I was thrilled! There was a little dog called Moujik who I felt was not too keen on me being there. I remember the thick air of cigarette smoke and perfume, rolls of fabric bursting with exotic colors, pots stuffed with coloring pencils, piles of sketches messily placed on desks with fabric samples clipped on them. I was little and I remember everyone being big and the crazy busy-ness of grown-ups dressed up with lipstick and painted nails. That was my first taste of YSL, and who would have known that at sixteen I would be transported back to that same studio on avenue Marceau, but this time not wearing a fairy dress but being fitted for a Haute Couture wedding dress for an Yves show. I remember both Yves and I being quite shy of one another. He would always greet me

very sweetly and call me "ma petite Lucie." We would then have these awkward kisses at the end of the runway in front of all the press. We would literally hold on to each other and he would fumble around with my veil, we would turn to each other and kiss, sometimes on the lips, other times a peck on the cheek. I could tell from the first time I made this journey with Yves that it was not easy for him, and I could feel his anxiety throughout the ordeal, so out of instinct I held him tight. It was Yves's sensitive side that I felt most connected to. We spoke a lot through the eyes when we found ourselves in these stressful fashion moments together. The big joy for me was being in the room, being fitted, tweaked and examined in Haute Couture by such a master. It's such a memory: you felt the talent, the eye. He just knew what the dress needed or did not need. Magic was being made and it felt so incredible. I had many of these behind-the-scenes experiences, seeing creative moments unfold— and getting told off for "not standing up tall! Being fitted for my real wedding dress, after having married Yves each season, I thought a miracle. I actually got to get married for real. I was planning a very relaxed country wedding and Yves sketched a gypsy-style dress for me with pockets in the skirt where I could put a hanky when things got too emotional. So there I am standing in my dress at my final fitting; Loulou was getting ready to place my veil and out jumps Moujik, **Yves's dog,** and bites my mother's leg! Not the best moment! What do I do? Rushing to my mother, I realized the concern in the room was for the dress, not for my mother's leg! My last memory of Yves is at my father's funeral, and I was so touched that he was there. Of course, it was his **love** for Loulou and him wanting to be close to her at such a sad time. A few years later I find myself next to Loulou grieving the loss of Yves. And four years later I am standing in the same church grieving for Loulou. The greats are going and I feel such joy and gratitude at being part of their very cool gang,

YSL, Paris, 1984

Sayoko Yamaguchi, Tracy Leigh, Paris, October 1982

YSL, Paris, November 1995

Tracy Leigh, Paris, March 1983

Kirat, Violetta Sanchez, Paris, October 1983

YSL, Amalia Vairelli, Haute Couture, Paris, January 1989

Paris, January 1989

Paris, October 1983

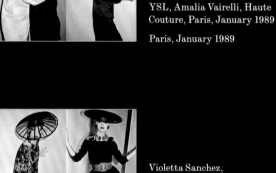

Violetta Sanchez, Paris, March 1984

Linda Evangelista, Paris, October 1986

Pat Cleveland, Paris, October 1983

Anne Rohart, Kirat, YSL model, Paris, October 1984

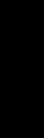

Pat Cleveland, Haute Couture, Paris, January 1989

Lisa Rutledge, Tracy Leigh, Paris, October 1982

Tracy Leigh, Haute Couture, Paris, January 1982

Sayoko Yamaguchi, Paris, March 1983/84

Pat Cleveland, Paris, March 1983/84

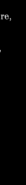

Veronica Webb, Paris, October 1986

Jerry Hall, Monsieur Alexandre, Paris, March 1984

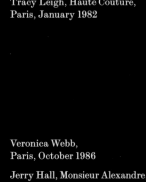

Jerry Hall, Talita,
Paris, October 1979

Laetitia Casta, YSL,
Haute Couture,
Paris, 1999

Alice Dodd,
Haute Couture,
Paris, January 1995

Alva Chinn (left),
YSL, YSL model,
Opium Party,
New York, 1978

Ewa Meissner (right),
Haute Couture,
Paris, January 1992

Violetta Sanchez,
Gloria Burgess,
Mounia, YSL model,
Paris, March 1984

Amalia Vairelli, Paris

Dootie, Nicole
Dorier, YSL model,
Paris, October 1980

Claudia Mason,
Haute Couture,
Paris, July 1991

Iman,
Paris, March 1984

Lorelei, Haute Couture,
Paris, July 1985

Mounia, Paris

Esther Cañadas,
Paris, October 1999

YSL, Sadiye Guéye,
Paris, 1988

Stella Tennant,
Haute Couture,
Paris, January 1993

Sonia Cole, Paris

Iman,
Paris, October 1983

Natalia Zavillova,
Anna Maria Cseh,
Haute Couture,
Paris, July 1999

Jerry Hall, YSL model,
Paris, October 1980

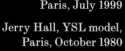

Paris, October 1987

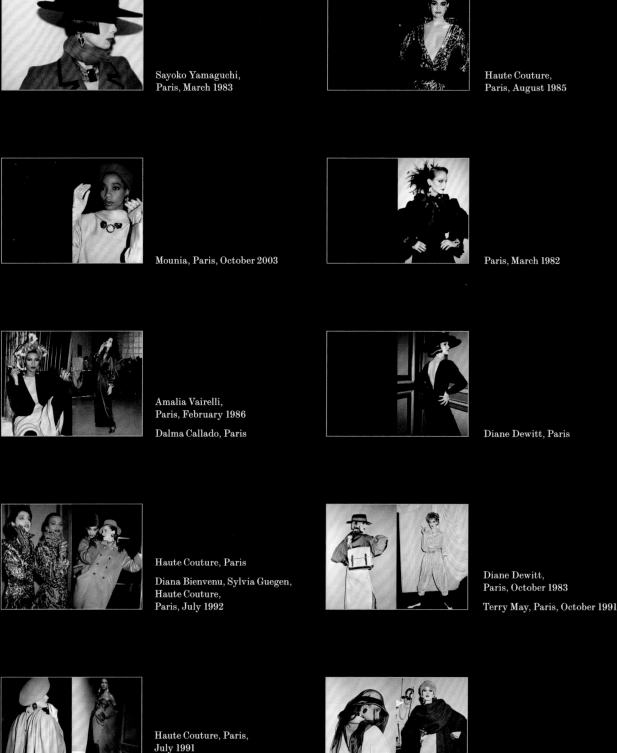

Sayoko Yamaguchi,
Paris, March 1983

Haute Couture,
Paris, August 1985

Mounia, Paris, October 2003

Paris, March 1982

Amalia Vairelli,
Paris, February 1986

Dalma Callado, Paris

Diane Dewitt, Paris

Haute Couture, Paris

Diana Bienvenu, Sylvia Guegen,
Haute Couture,
Paris, July 1992

Diane Dewitt,
Paris, October 1983

Terry May, Paris, October 1991

Haute Couture, Paris,
July 1991

Katoucha Niane, Haute
Couture, Paris, July 1991

Paris, March 1984

Paris, March 1981

Shalom Harlow, Haute Couture,
Paris, January 1993

Amber Valletta,
Paris, March 1993

Dalma Callado,
Paris, March 1983

Jerry Hall, Paris

YSL,
Paris, October 1995

YSL, Loulou
de La Falaise,
Paris, October 1979

Pat Cleveland,
Paris, October 1983

Dalma Callado,
Paris

Violetta Sanchez,
Paris, October 1984

Paris, October 1983

YSL, Sayoko Yamaguchi,
Paris, 1983

Iman,
Paris, March 1982

Sayoko Yamaguchi,
Paris, March 1980

"Yves Saint Laurent,
25 Years of Design,"
Metropolitan
Museum of Art,
New York, December 1983

Pat Cleveland, Mounia,
Paris, 1978

Paris, October 1982

YSL model, Iman,
Paris, October 1983

Anna Bayle,
Haute Couture,
Paris, January 1989

Paris, October 1983

Amalia Vairelli,
Haute Couture,
Paris, January 1989

Paris, October 1983

Pat Cleveland,
Paris, October 1982

Mounia,
Paris, October 1980

YSL and his models,
Paris, October 1983

Paris, October 1986

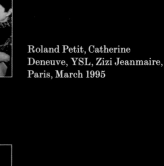

Roland Petit, Catherine
Deneuve, YSL, Zizi Jeanmaire,
Paris, March 1995

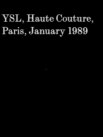

YSL, Haute Couture,
Paris, January 1989

YSL, Karl Lagerfeld,
5th Anniversary, Le Palace,
Paris, March 1983

Diana Vreeland, Costume
Institute opening, Metropolitan
Museum of Art, New York, 1980

YSL, Diana Vreeland,
Metropolitan Museum of Art,
New York, 1983

YSL, Karl Lagerfeld,
Paris, 1982

Pierre Bergé, YSL

Antonio Lopez, YSL

YSL, New York,
December 1983

Grace Jones, Grace Jones,
Le Palace, Paris, 1981

YSL, Paloma Picasso,
Le Palace, Paris, October 1982

Betty Catroux,
Paris, March 2001

Loulou de La Falaise, YSL

YSL, Nan Kempner,
New York, January 1999

Catherine Deneuve,
Paris, 1988

Carla Bruni,
Haute Couture,
Paris, July 1995

Karen Mulder,
Haute Couture,
Pairs, July 1995

YSL

Sayoko Yamaguchi,
Paris, March 1980

YSL,
Paris, October 1995

A model and YSL,
Paris, October 1980

YSL, Metropolitan
Museum of Art,
New York, 1983

Mounia,
Haute Couture,
Paris, January 1983

YSL, Mounia,
Paris, October 1980

Paris, October 1980

Lucie de La Falaise,
Haute Couture,
Paris, July 1990

Violetta Sanchez,
Paris, March 1984

Kirat, YSL,
Haute Couture,
Paris, July 1985

Jerry Hall,
Paris, October 1980

Pat Cleveland,
Paris, March 1983

YSL in his office,
Paris, 1984

Karen Mulder,
Haute Couture,
Paris, July 1995

Paris, March 1982

Haute Couture,
Paris, September 1988

Dalma Callado,
Paris

Katoucha Niane,
Haute Couture,
Paris, July 1991

Heather Stewart-
Whyte, Haute Couture,
Paris, January 1992

Tatiana Sorokko,
Paris, October 1992

Tatiana Sorokko,
Haute Couture,
Paris, January 1992

Kate Moss,
Haute Couture,
Paris, January 1993

Shalom Harlow,
Haute Couture,
Paris, January 1993

Natalia Kretova,
Haute Couture,
Paris, January 1993

Karen Mulder,
Haute Couture,
Paris, July 1991

Leatitia Casta,
Haute Couture,
Paris, January 2000

Beverly Peele,
Paris, March 1992

Alice Dodd,
Paris

YSL, Amalia Vairelli,
Paris, March 1991

Kirat,
Haute Couture,
Paris, July 1984

Pat Cleveland,
Haute Couture,
Paris, January 1986

Mounia,
Haute Couture,
Paris, January 1985

YSL model, Paris

Violetta Sanchez,
Paris, March 1984

Lucie de La Falaise,
Haute Couture,
Paris, July 1991

YSL model,
Paris

YSL, Loulou de La
Falaise and models,
Paris, October 1984

Katoucha Niane,
Haute Couture,
Paris, January 1988

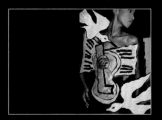

YSL and models,
Paris, March 1985

ACKNOWLEDGMENTS

Yves: you were a genius, an innovator; you changed the world of fashion, and kept the fantasy alive.
Pierre Bergé: thank you for the lovely foreword.

The amazing support from the following people made this book possible . . .

Thanks to those who wrote:
Betty Catroux, Pat Cleveland, Catherine Deneuve, Jerry Hall, Grace Jones, Lucie de La Falaise,
Paloma Picasso, and Valerie Steele.

Thank you, I couldn't have done it without you:
Shoko Takayasu, Vanessa Salle, Jesse Frohman, John Granito, Sarah Montague, Beatrice Dupire, Arturo
Stanig, Brian Saltzman, Joanne Artese, Antonio Lopez, and Jeff Chu.

Thanks to my editor, Christopher Sweet of Thames & Hudson, for believing in my vision.

Thanks to the most fabulous design team:
Fabien Baron, Brian Hetherington, Alicia Shreders, and Maxime Poiblanc from Baron & Baron.

Thanks to my agents, Celeste Fine and Caitlin McDonald of Sterling Lord Literistic.

Thanks also to
Philippe Mugnier and Olivier Flaviano from Fondation Pierre Bergé-Yves Saint Laurent,
Véronique Lefèvre Sweet,
Photographers Limited Editions (Vienna), Steven Kasher Gallery (New York), and Izzy Gallery (Toronto).

On the cover:
Front: Roxanne Lowit, Yves Saint Laurent, Metropolitan Museum of Art, New York, 1983.
Back: Roxanne Lowit, Jerry Hall, Paris, October 1995.

First published in 2014 in the United States of America by Thames & Hudson Inc.,
500 Fifth Avenue, New York, New York 10110

First published in 2014 in the United Kingdom by Thames & Hudson Ltd, 181A High Holborn,
London WC1V 7QX

This compact edition first published in 2020

Reprinted in 2023

Library of Congress Control Number 2019934258

British Library Cataloguing-in-Publication Data: A catalogue record for this book is available
from the British Library

ISBN 978-0-500-02303-7

Printed and bound in China

Be the first to know about our new releases,
exclusive content and author events by visiting
thamesandhudson.com
thamesandhudsonusa.com
thamesandhudson.com.au